POEMS
of
SORTS

POEMS
of
SORTS

Bob Rutzel

Poems of Sorts

Copyright © 2019 by Bob Rutzel. All rights reserved.

No part of this publication may be reproduced, stored in a retrieval system or transmitted in any way by any means, electronic, mechanical, photocopy, recording or otherwise without the prior permission of the author except as provided by USA copyright law.

The opinions expressed by the author are not necessarily those of URLink Print and Media.

1603 Capitol Ave., Suite 310 Cheyenne, Wyoming USA 82001
1-888-980-6523 | admin@urlinkpublishing.com

URLink Print and Media is committed to excellence in the publishing industry.

Book design copyright © 2019 by URLink Print and Media. All rights reserved.

Published in the United States of America

ISBN 978-1-64367-384-4 (Paperback)
ISBN 978-1-64367-383-7 (Digital)

29.04.19

Acknowledgments

I have been writing short stories for many years, and the proof of all that can be found in many trash cans. Now poems or thoughts in rhyme or free verse are a leap of faith for me, and hopefully some will be enjoyed.

The interest in writing started many years ago by reading *The October Country* by Ray Bradbury. It's a collection of short stories, and I liked the way he said things. Lately, poems have been uppermost in my mind, but I also write movie reviews for some friends and install the reviews on IMDb.

The high school class of 1960 in Syosset, New York, had probably one of the best English teachers ever in Ron Barry. Also, Mr. Barry encouraged all of us regardless of the area we wanted to participate in.

Others who have encouraged me:

Niece: Krystyn (Rutzel) Serrano, who needs to put her life experiences on paper.

Friend: Annita-Tex Sours, who also needs to put her life experiences on paper.

John Delin (my captain from the Safety Patrol back in the day) who operates Ken Again, a poetry e-mag for those who want to contribute their poems.

Bob Thomas, author of Golf Books including Ben Hogan's Secret, who told me to always keep things simple and maintain a sense of humor.

Grateful for all help regardless where it came from.

MY POEMS BY DESIGN

by Bob Rutzel

I have always maintained that I would like to do nothing but write. Long gone is the dream of pitching for the New York Yankees.

Many of my poems or thoughts deal with thoughts that, I think, most of us have from time to time. These are thoughts that I have, and I do think about often especially those about life, death, dreams, and so on. There is nothing new regarding these thoughts. Only difference is that I wrote about them the way I see them.

I have tried to do poems with tongue in cheek, a little humor if it came easy, and then put some truth in it so it will have some meaning.

Why the poem format? Prose takes too long to get to the point. The reader has to go through a lot of text. Poetry is simpler, easy to see the beginning, middle, and ending. Hopefully, the reader won't get bored.

Samuel Taylor Coleridge once said that poetry is "the best words in the best order." I have tried to stay faithful to that wisdom.

What about rhyming? Some poems may not be conducive to rhymes. I have found that sometimes a rhyme will occur within a poem for a short time and then revert back to nonrhyme (ha, it almost sounds like poems have a life of their own). Rhyme or free verse, it's the thought that counts most.

Sometimes a rhyme may come about like a hook in a song. I do not concern myself with trying to get something to rhyme. If it happens, it happens.

    One of the things I especially like about the poem format is that poetry should be read aloud as it has more impact that way and once spoken aloud, I believe, it is easier to understand.

POEMS OF SORTS
SOME RHYME,
SOME DON'T

HAPPY

Recently, someone asked me
: if I was happy. I said I was happy when Mickey Mantle was playing baseball.
: if I get angry. Sometimes.
: if I cry. Every day.
: if I have hope. Always.
: if I pray. All the time
: if I could go back in time, when? When Mickey Mantle was playing baseball.

PERFECT DAY

How well and wry a day is
this that creeps, almost sleeps.
A day too old for one so young
for this day has just begun.
The minutes, the hours
have not the powers
to rush the slowest-closing flowers.
The day drags and drags and come what may
the day, this day, will stay as it is:
Perfect.

TWO POEMS

I completed two poems.
The words came so fast, you see;
I had no choice says me.
And to write in the glow
of a light so bright
I couldn't see what I was saying,
and I was hoping and praying
the words
made some sense.

SNOWING

From the warm, I watched it snow
and saw flakes blindly go
until the white blanket was complete.
Oh, what a magical treat.
Then it stopped
and lay quiet and still,
and it took a while until
the only sound
was the shovel in the whitish ground.
Yet the snow will come once more,
and I will watch as before
as the flakes slowly cover the ground
with a magic so easily found.

CHRISTMAS MORNING

'Twas hours after, you know.
All was done, no place to go.
The presents were stacked on the side.
The wrappings no longer hid what was inside.
Yes, a bit of a mess, you see,
but a merry time had we.
And, we didn't want it to end.
so we let the mess blend
as part of the room,
no sight of the broom.
And so we rested for a bit,
knowing that it will make
a fine memory.

THE REMOTE

The most important job in life
is to control the TV Remote.
Controlling the Remote solves everything,
all is good and there are no obstacles.
Lose control of the Remote and we are lost,
never to be found or heard from ever again.
So we must do everything in our power to
control the Remote.
After all, the Remote is the most the most
important invention ever made and it must be
safeguarded.
Controlling the Remote allows us to live
our lives in complete harmony,
otherwise, we will be lost and never
heard from ever again.
Today we control the TV room,
Tomorrow . . .
well . . . you know.

WHEN I RETIRED

I noticed that work to be done now
—can be done tomorrow.
Sleeping late
—is rule number 1.
Youth isn't wasted on the young,
—their energy is.
Watching a clock is a wonderful time machine
—where time is forgotten,
but I also noticed that the grass
—won't wait for tomorrow.

A BIRTHDAY

is a moment in time
celebrated moments later
in terms of years.
When looked back on,
birthdays employ the past and the present
at the same time.
And the spaces they occupy
change so often to such a point
we do not know if we can
rely on our memories
to put those moments
in the correct order.
But the next birthday is when
we take stock
to see how we fare
and regardless of what is seen,
we vow to do better because
we can always do that.

GETTING OLD

I think I am getting old.
Isn't memory one of the first things to go?
Now, I'm talking small things
that may add up later to be big.
Right now, I forget where I put the car keys;
did I turn the light off downstairs or
tell myself I am coming right back?
Did I lock the outside door? Did I put the cat out?
Wait a minute, I don't have a cat
I think I am getting better already.

LET ME TELL YOU SOMETHING

Inspired by my niece Krystyn

Let me tell you something:
I and a lot of other people used to say the Days go by too fast.
But let me tell you something again: that was not exactly right.
The Weeks go by too fast now.
But let me tell you something else:
I hope I do not ever say the Months are going by too fast.
But let me tell you one last thing:
I hope I never, ever, say the Years are going by too fast.
But let me tell you the really last and true thing:
LIFE is going by too fast.

SOME CALL ME

Some call me Bob, Bobby, Mr. Bob,
Old Coot, Rutz, Mr. Rutzel, Dude.
I say I am all the above,
but still always . . .
a child traveling alone
as are we all.

DINNER PARTY?

You want to invite me to a dinner party?
You know I don't like going out at night
and spending time with people I don't know.
That is not my idea of a good time.
I have things to do and am quite tired.
I don't have time for this.
Do you realize all I would have to do?
I would have to shave, and shower, of course,
comb my hair, brush my teeth and floss,
shine shoes, and put on clean clothes.
It all takes time, you know.
Will need another shower when I return,
No, I do not like going out at night.
Maybe another time, all right?
Cake?
I'll be right over.

A CHILD AGAIN

If I were a child again,
oh, the wisdom I would impart
to one and all,
and I would start
by telling them I now know
what is true for me and for them.
Oh, what a time I would have
watching their eyes
look toward the skies,
hoping I would go away
and not make trouble on this or any day.
No, they would not then listen or believe,
and that's okay
for, in time, they will come to see
things unfold as they were meant to be.

REGRETS

I have many regrets.
Oh, you don't?
Think about that for a minute.
If your mother and father are gone,
did you do enough when they were here?
I did some things
but could have, should have
done more.
All I can do now
is say you do not have the time
you think you have.
Do it now.
Oh, your parents are still here?
Lucky you.

A CHILD'S EYES

We see the child looking at us
with smiling eyes, and
we see innocence,
unwavering trust,
happiness, joy,
and love.
What we don't see
Is God looking
through the child's eyes
at us, His creations.
As we marvel at the child,
He marvels at us
for a time until
the child's eyes
cloud by seeing the world
another way.

Q & A

When I was a boy, the doctor would ask:
Did you ever have this?
I said: No.
In my 20s, the doctor would ask:
Did you ever have this?
I said:
No. The same answer applied throughout my
30s, 40s, and 50s.
Now when the doctor asks that kind of question,
I say:
Not yet.

IT'S HAPPENED BEFORE

I think everything that has happened in the world
has happened before.
This would explain prophecy, savants,
and history repeating.
The mind never dies, but rests,
comes back, and remembers.
Now what is the reason for these recurring lives?
Is someone playing a game and looking to see
different outcomes?

A LAWN

There is nothing better-looking
than a nicely cut lawn.
So crisp, so clean
with slight undulations
that make your head sway
to such point you can see the
swells and waves that continue
to roll, and roll, and roll.
I could watch it all day.
I cut it, look at it, savor it, and then
wait until it needs cutting again.
I like looking at a nicely cut lawn.

FRIENDS

It's not exactly that they think like you.
Some will, some won't.
It's not exactly that they do things you like.
Some will, some won't.
Then exactly what is it?
It's a great respect for each other.
Exactly.

ON DEATH AND HEAVEN

The older we get,
the more we think of death.
It will happen and I
do not want to know when.
Woody Allen said he didn't want
to be there when it happened.
Somerset Maugham said he thought
an exception would be made in his case.
So I made a decision:
I will embrace both comments above,
knowing full well neither will make
any difference.
But I will keep in mind what Frank Sinatra said:
The best is yet to come.

WHAT IS TIME?

Time is the duration interval between:
this and that,
here and there,
point A and point B,
up and down,
in and out,
opening and closing,
beginning and ending,
a single moment to infinity.
Basically, it's how long it takes something
 to complete.
What is "long?"
A variable of time.
But Time can also be a stopping point,
a specific instance.
How do I know?
Easy.
It's time for me to finish this poem.
I have stopped.
It's Time.

DECISIONS WHEN I RETIRED

I woke up and asked myself:
What should I do today?
Wear this or that?
Should I go here or there?
Do this or that?
Eat out or stay in?
See this person or that person?
Go to this store or that one?
Work in the yard or do it another day?
You know . . . waking up
shouldn't be so problematic.

SHORT-TERM MEMORY

I realized I had a problem
as I couldn't remember
what happened a few moments ago.
Now I have the solution and know
what to do about it.
Ahhh . . . here we go . . .

GROWING OLD

I took some time to remember
when I worked overseas
in Saudi Arabia.
It's been so long ago that it almost seems like a dream,
and that it never really happened.
I hunted down pictures I took.
And those shots did convince me that "yes, I was there."
Is this what happens when we grow older, whereby
the past seems vaguely like a dream or dream-like?
But I have now learned the secret to knowing the Past,
okay, my Past:
Take a camera with me wherever I go.

UP CLOSE AND PERSONAL

Up close and personal information
should not be allowed.
Let me see the race, game, or what have you
and be done with it.
A while back I wanted Golfer A to win.
Then the announcer started to talk about Golfer B.
Well, Golfer B had a very sad story.
Now I wanted Golfer B to win.
See?

10 MOST ANNOYING THINGS

Everything. Everything. Everything.
Everything. Everything. Everything.
Everything. Everything. Everything
Everything. HA!
Hey, I have my moments too.

LOSS

by Bob Rutzel

When it wasn't working out with me,
she said:
What have you lost?
I said:
Everything.

AND STILL MORE POEMS

MARRIAGE

I know someone who
never married.
He asked the same girl 3-times.
No was the answer 3-times.
He says he always thought he would be good at it.
Now he doesn't bother.
When he sees elderly couples,
he cringes,
not wanting anything to do
with that scene.
Still . . .
he says he has moments whereby
he wishes
the answer was yes.

IT'S HOT

A hot August night,
The power is out.
Oh, it's hot, hot, hot,
hotter than hot.
It's cool . . . not, not, not.
What can be done?
What? What? What?
It's hot, hot, hot.
Do you hear?
It's hotter than hot.
Something needs to be done,
but what? What? What? What?
You tell me to sit still and let
a breeze come to me.
That's all you got?
Hey, it's hot, hotter than hot.
Okay, I'll try, try, try.
But why, why, why
does it have to be so
hot, hot, hot. Need that power to come back, back, back
Now!

TEMPORARY BLOCKAGE

If One considers Oneself a writer
and has nothing to write about
what does One do?
Let's not call it Writer's Block
as that implies there is a subject
but no avenue to handle it . . . yet.
Let's call it a blockage.
One does know that this is only temporary,
and all will come loose and flow soon . . . but
just when . . .
the One does not know.
Something is missing—perhaps a Muse.
Where does one go to find a Muse?
There should be a Muse Store
around somewhere.
As soon as the One finds one,
the ink will flow once more.

HEAVEN

What if we get to Heaven
and discover some of our dearest friends
are not there.
We knew them to be good in life;
a good brother, sister, husband, wife.
Friends to all but still not there.
We reason they are there, but under
another identity from perhaps a past life
we knew nothing about
and are not recognizable to us.
Those friends may be there and see that
we are not there and also may assume we have another identity they knew nothing about. Some conundrum we all may have But Heaven shouldn't be so complicated unless it is using a page from Witness Protection for reasons we can never fathom. Or simply put, they may not be there at all. How will we know?

THAT SPECIAL LOOK

We all know the look we like in a girl.
The look that makes our knees buckle
the mouth go dry
and incoherent sentences abound.
We cannot get that image out of our head.
That is, until another girl comes along with
that same look, and the knees buckle
and the mouth dries up
and gives rise gibberish utterings.
And so it is
and here we are,
but wait . . .
we see another girl
with that same special look,
the knees again buckle . . .
Oh, it just never ends,
does it?

A REAL CONCERN

The old man sat waiting
for his family.
He knows they are coming
because it's his birthday.
If he told them his concerns
They would laugh at him
for being silly,
but the records show
that many elderly
people die at or near
their birthdays. The old man realizes
he has no choice
and just needs to live a while
longer beyond this day.
He vows to give it a shot,
and hope for the best
as he continues to wait.

THE ANSWER

The World, Life, Death.
Suppose one day
it all gets "figured" out.
Then what?
What will change?
Nothing.
Nothing because
whoever "figures" it all out
will be very wrong.

BIRTHDAY CARDS

Sometimes finding the perfect card
is not possible.
We search and search and refuse to settle.
We vow to come back another day
as then that card may—hopefully—appear.
When we do find the perfect card
we buy all copies.
and send when that applies.
The problem can arise when
the same card is sent to close
family members.
"Hey, you sent the same card to
my sister. Why did I get the same one?"
The answer is simple:
because it was the perfect card.

DIFFICULT POETRY

Reading difficult poetry
Can be exasperating
When one realizes one does
Not know as well as one should
—at least—
A little something about:
History, literature, folklore, myths,
Music, science, sports, the arts, and so on.
Aren't you glad
That doesn't apply here?

1943 COPPER PENNY

Back in the day
copper was used for WWII efforts.
Various accounts say that low copper
quantities were produced for coins.
We were told that if we found
a 1943 copper penny, we would
get a new Thunderbird from Ford.
So what did we do?
We went to see the new Thunderbirds, of course.
Oh, yes, it will be ours soon. Count on it.
Really beautiful. Can't wait.
We found a 1943 copper penny.
We called a coin dealer in NY City,
who said to give it the magnet test.
If it attracts, you have a zinc penny.
It attracted.
Are there any 1943 copper pennies out there?
Heaven only knows.
I think if we ever did find an actual
1943 copper penny that we would
get more than the value of a new T-Bird.
Still looking . . .

HIGH SCHOOL REUNIONS

High school reunions sound nice.
Yeah, let's see old friends again,
that would be good, and find out
what is going on with them.
Yes, but that should be only for
one, maybe two reunions.
After that, it becomes too sad.
Reunions, if staged too many times, will have
fewer and fewer attendees.
That is sad, very sad.
Sad but true.
Every reunion has those remembrance
pictures on a big screen and tears are shed and it is here
that we think one day our name and picture will be included.
Having one or two reunions will capture almost everyone
that everyone will want to see,
and remembrance pictures will be few or not at all.
And isn't that a better picture of what a true reunion
should be about?
After the 2nd Reunion,
Forgetaboutit.

WEIGHT LOSS

I ran into an old friend yesterday.
I should say he ran into me
as I didn't recognize him at all.
I remember him as a 300+ something pounder.
I had to ask: how did you lose the weight?
He says he found a foolproof method.
Says he exercised more, a lot more.
"And it's all worth it, can't you see?"
What's the secret? I had to ask.
He tells me portion control and he exercised
in front of a full-length mirror every other day
NAKED.
Says every day is too exhausting and the body
needs time to recover.
I could stand to lose a few pounds.
Lord knows I tried everything else, but
does it have to be a full-length
mirror?

MY SCALE

I am fine,
but I think my scale is
gaining weight.
I knew it was heavy
when I first bought it,
but somehow it has gotten
out of hand and lost control.
I do not know where it goes
when I am not around,
but as soon as I show up,
I see more pounds in the display.
What to do? What to do?
I could buy another scale and
hope it's more disciplined.
Who am I kidding?
These scales
are all the same and do whatever
whenever they want and
with whomever they want.
It's just sad to know I am
a favorite target right now.
Very sad.

SHE SHAVED HER HEAD

She still looks good, but
looks like a chemo patient.
She doesn't mind.
She knows why she did it, and
will tell anyone who has the courage
to ask.
It was vanity, she claims.
She was super obsessed with
making sure her lush blonde hair
was always in place and presented
the best view for others to see.
Over time, it was just too much
keeping up appearances.
It tired her. Really tired her.
So this was the solution.
She knows she can regrow
her luscious blonde hair, and not
spend as much time caring for it as before,
But just not now.
Does she have regrets?
Sometimes.

THOSE GONE

Deceased family and friends.
Yes, we still miss them.
Gone too soon,
and we lost the connection
but keep them alive in our memories.
It's not enough,
but it's all we have
until we meet them again
and make new
memories.

MAKING A CORRECTION

My friend G told me he went back in time
to solve problem and make the correct
decision he should have made back then.
Me: Did you make the change?
No, I couldn't.
Me: But you had all the information,
parameters, etc.
Something happened. My mind-set was the same
as it was originally.
Me: What does that mean?
I couldn't see the future.

FATHERS' DAY

Sometimes a father's special day
doesn't turn out the expected way.
Friends will always ask,
"So what did the kids get you?"
Smiling, my father replied, "The kids got Helen
a TV for the kitchen."
And he's more than okay with that.

HUNGER

Dieters can never understand
when nondieters are asked,
"Are you hungry?"
The reply, "not really"
really rankles dieters,
who always have the reply,
"I can eat" at the ready.
But to be polite, dieters
will sometimes also reply with, "not really"
and just know they will die if they don't
get something soon.

KIDSSAY . . .

A touch of lemon:
At a famous seafood restaurant
niece Elizabeth took her lemon and started
to squeeze it over her plate, missing
the fish entirely.
I shout, "Over the fish, the fish, the fish!"
She shouts back, "I will, I will, I will."
Next up: nephew Ryan:
I am setting up a computer system
at my brother's house.
Ryan, at 4-yrs of age, comes in
and starts touching things.
I say, "Don't touch anything."
Ryan continues to touch things.
I ask, "Do you have any money?"
He says no.
"If you break anything, how are you going to pay for it?"
Silence.
Finally, he says, "When are you going home?"

THE VALUE OF $5.00

Regardless of my age, my grandfather, Leon,
would give me $5.00 for Christmas and birthdays.
It was always $5.00 and I always thanked him.
It wasn't until my late teens that I realized
I was thanking him because he knew the value
of money and he was going to imprint this value on to me.
He came here from Poland with nothing,
worked hard, and did okay for himself and his family.
That $5.00 reminded him when he was my age that he
never received anything regardless of the occasion,
and for someone to give him $5.00, he would be
considered rich.
Yes, he never forgot that he never received anything.
Times have changed and I used to give my nieces and nephews
a standard sum, more than $5.00.
And they did thank me, wishing it was more, I am sure.
But now I have reconsidered and now will only give $5.00.
Yes, the times have changed, and are here to stay,
but imprinting some values are important.

111 AND 1111

The above numbers occur to me most often.
I have no idea what they mean, if indeed,
there is any meaning at all.
I thought they might be references in the Bible,
but that didn't work out.
If I open a book, see a license plate, or even look
at a clock, one of those numbers will show up.
Why?
I have asked around, and no one seems to have any clue,
and most have never heard of such a thing, or so they tell me.
Yes, some back off as though I was contagious.
Should I use I Ching?
Play them in Vegas or in a lottery or go to a fortune-teller?
Where do I go to find the answer?
Maybe in dreams? Hmmmm . . .
I will think of these numbers before I go to sleep
And see what happens.
So far nothing has happened.
Stay tuned. This isn't over.

YARD TOOLS

I enter the tool shack,
and I hear the implements call out to me.
The **saw** sings: Pick me, pick me. You know
there are trees within trees that need to be cut.
The **Rake** cries out: Pick me, pick me. You know
there is much hay you left on the lawn.
The **shovel** grits and says: Pick me, pick me.
You need to fill in some holes with dirt.
The **Clippers,** in a snippy way, says: Pick me, pick me.
You know there are tree limbs that need cutting back.
The **Ladder,** in a matter-of-fact manner, says: Pick me, pick me.
You know you need to get up there to clean out the gutters.
The **Lawnmower** smiles and knows it will be picked as it has a seat.
I take the lawnmower out amid the cries of those "pick me" tools
as they are still clamoring for my attention as I ride out, but
they know I'll be back for them soon, one at a time,
just not now.

THAT LITTLE BIRD

The little bird who could not yet fly
was not afraid of the lawnmower engine noise.
It didn't know what danger is and what might happen to it.
The little bird just walked around as if it was all alone.
I cut the engine off and the little bird just stood there
as if nothing happened.
I was sure the mother was watching.
I put the engine back on and the noise still didn't rattle
the little bird.
Still no sign of the mother.
I moved away, much to the mother's delight, I am sure.
We were once like that little bird.
What happened to us that we fear almost everything?
In time, that little bird will become like us.
Poor bird.

GRASS AND CHURCH

Cutting the grass once a week
is like going to church once a week
every week.
Both must be done.
Don't cut the grass and we get 2-things:
Taller grass and guilt.
Don't go to church each week gives us
a major guilt that must be atoned.
Now, in winter, the grass doesn't grow,
but the church is still there
every week . . .
summer and winter.

WHA' HAPPENED?

After a pretty good weekend,
I wake up on Monday morning,
get my coffee,
check my e-mail,
turn around,
and the next thing I know,
it's Friday afternoon.
Wha' happened?

WHY ARE WE HERE?

Many of us have wondered
"Why am I here?"
As for me, I do not wonder
about that.
I do not care.
As long as I know that YOU picked
me for some special purpose
I am good with that.
That is all I need to know.
However, if YOU decide to tell me,
I'm listening.

MUST BE PERFECT

In my life, as in all our lives,
Chaos, problems, difficult decisions
Reign at times.
I have countered those things with
Some things I can control
And they must be perfect:
Pens, envelopes, eggs, stamps, coffee.
In the great scheme of things,
They don't seem to amount to much,
But they help me get through life.

MORE POEMS OF SORTS
SOME RHYME, SOME DON'T

WORK

My uncle owned a farm.
In summer, after I got back from work,
I would ask him, "What did you do today?"
He would sometimes reply, "Nothing. Too hot."
In winter, I would ask the same and get,
"Nothing. Too cold."
Retired, I now have the farm and believe
I am becoming my uncle.

SNOW

Sometimes snow
descends like white rain pellets,
or heavy large white patches,
or regular-sized flakes,
or blinding whiteouts.
Snow can come
straight down,
slanted,
in waves,
fast or slow.
Yes, snow and we have a jolly
good time with all this.
But no matter
when all is done
we still need the shovel.
Then it's not
so much fun.

MY HOME PLANET

When things go wrong,
I usually tell people
that I need to find my home planet
because things that go wrong here
do not go wrong there.
How do I know all this?
I am not sure, but I just know.
I don't know where my home planet is,
and I am trying to give this one a chance,
but it is taking too long.
No one understands the wrongs inflicted.
All they understand is that everyone
is fair game,
but not them.

NAMING THE BABY

Inspired by Mary-Joan C.

The mother-in-law was upset
with her daughter-in-law
for not naming her baby daughter after a saint.
The mother-in-law asked,
"Why didn't you name her after a saint?"
To which the daughter-in-law replied,
"We'll make her a Saint."

BAD MOOD

I went to the post office,
and the clerk asked,
"And how are you today?"
I said I was fine, "but if I came
in here yesterday, I would have
bitten your head off."
"Well," the clerk says, "I am glad
you are better today."
We finished up the transaction,
and as I was leaving, the clerk says,
"Thank you for not coming in yesterday."

THOSE PAPERS

When my grandfather's friend opened
his wallet and I saw all those important papers inside,
I was shocked.
His wallet must have been at least 3-inches thick,
maybe more.
I was just a kid, but
I asked myself,
would I
know how
and when
and where
to get
all of those important papers later in life?
And if I couldn't, what would happen to me?

BACK TO THE STORE

I have no memory of this, but
my aunt used to tell me that my mother
would often send me back to the store
because I got the wrong item.
My mother is gone now, and I wish
I had the opportunity
to be sent again
to the store
and get the right item for her.

MY MOTHER

I used to believe my mother was
not always right.
She would tell me what
I did wrong,
that I should have done this
and not that.
She would raise her voice
a little,
shake her head,
and look hurt,
saying she just couldn't
understand me.
It is only now that I know,
I was the one who wasn't right.
Why did it take so long to see that?

ADVICE

I wasn't bad as a kid,
although I did have
opportunities.
But it was something
my father once told me
many years ago
that set me straight
for the rest of my life
He said:
"Don't ever let me
answer for anything
you have done."

A SCENT

Looking for a pencil
I opened a drawer,
and there I saw
a red stick
with the unmistakable scent of crayons.
And I was back in
first grade,
coloring the letters of the alphabet,
and next in my bedroom coloring Trigger in Roy's book;
and then in the second grade, we were told
we would be making posters but not
with crayons.
I have no memory of how we did the posters.
All I know is that the crayon scent activated
a time machine into my past
for those good times.

POEMS AND SONGS

Who likes long poems?
No one likes long poems
unless they rhyme
and are catchy like
a jingle all the way through.
Songs are,
indeed,
poems too,
and if the melody
doesn't work,
with the words,
well, then . . .
it should remain
a poem.

UNDERSTANDING MEN

Inspired by Annita-Tex S.

We see and hear too often:
understanding Women.
This is the other side: the Man.
The Man finds a love, a true love,
and the Man will love this woman forever
because the Heart is deeply invested.
But let's say the woman, over time, changes
and becomes a Bitch.
A real Bitch.
The Man will still love this woman
forever because the Heart remembers
what it wants.
So now you understand what
the Man is all about.
But now the Man will stay
out of her way.

UNDERSTANDING WOMEN

Understanding women
has been tried since
Caveman days.
It simply cannot be done.
And this is why we see pictures
of a Caveman
dragging a woman by her hair.
The Caveman has come up
with the only solution
that works for him.
With the passage of time,
Modern Man has
no recourse but to
give in and think
of another time when
he was
a Caveman.

SOUL MATE

I often have dreams about
my soul mate.
She is very pretty,
smart,
well mannered,
friendly,
loyal,
with loving eyes.
But here's the thing:
I live in Virginia.
She lives in an underground bunker
on Mars.
Why do I have these
dreams?

SIMPLE POEMS

Yes, my poems are simple,
and quite easy to understand.
I am writing for you and for me,
and not for a poet historian/literary buff,
who, when they write, send all to
the dictionary, thesaurus,
or both.
Clint Eastwood says he makes movies
because he wants to see them.
I, too, want to see what I wrote.
That's on me.

WEATHERMEN

The weatherman said:
Rain today.
It didn't rain.
Next day he said:
4-inches of snow.
We saw no snow.
And the next day he said:
Clear and Sunny.
That's when we got the 4-inches of snow.
Parents: Steer your kids to being weathermen.
They can be wrong 98% of the time
and still
keep their job.

LOTTERIES

When I started to play
the lotteries,
I was living large
in the land of
Finally!
Hey, it could happen.
Ya never know, and
why not me?
But truth be told
I live in the land of
MAYBE...

LONG POEMS

In order to write long
meaningful poems,
one must know how to
write short
meaningful poems.
How am I doing so far?

NEW YORKERS

New Yorkers are known for 2-things:
    If you have a problem,
we have a solution.
    If we see something wrong,
we have suggestions.

THINGS YOU NEVER WANT TO HEAR YOUR CONTRACTOR SAY

- Oh, oh
- It's too big
- It's too small
- Oh God
- This won't work
- What th—
- We have a problem
- I never ran into anything like this
- This won't go . . .
- I can't stop it from slipping out
- There is just no way . . .
- I need to bring someone in to consult
- That'll be extra
- That'll be a lot extra

DREAM CHOICES

Whether we remember dreams
or not, we do dream.
The problem is when we dream
about things that have not been
in our experience.
We have no clue
why we seem to fit in.
While in the dream,
we are quite comfortable,
but when we are awake,
we are clueless.
What is this all about?
Are we subconsciously seeing different
possibilities of our Heaven, and will we
choose one of them when we die?
Or will that decision
be made for us?

HORSE RACING FAN

Met Bud at the race track.
He helped us with the order
of things as one horse
(and its number) was
scratched.
And the number was not
to be used in the race.
Bud told us he had a friend
who used his house number
to bet for many years.
We asked if his friend ever won.
He replied, "No."
Bud said he advised his friend
to move.

PEOPLE IN DREAMS

When I dream,
I often see people
I know and trust.
But when I awake,
I have no clue who
these people are.
Who are they?
Why are they in
my dreams?
Is it possible
I am seeing old friends
from past lives?

LET'S MEET

Let's meet where
there is no light
yet where it's bright.
A place seemingly wrong
yet incredibly strong.
A place where words
are not needed
as that spark is heeded.
and lingers
forever and ever
in that instant
because we are led
to a place where
a simple look is all that
need be said.

THE BIRDS

The winter was brutally cold,
rainy, high winds, much snow and ice.
I watched the birds
looking for food.
They pecked and pecked,
but I don't know if their
motions got anything.
Then I believe I heard
a voice telling me to do
something.
Now, I buy birdseed.

11TH MOST ANNOYING THING

A woman is in the cashier's line
at the grocery store.
The clerk tallies everything
and tells the woman the total cost.
At this moment the woman
reaches into her handbag and
looks around for her wallet.
She finally finds it and then
proceeds to count out the money.
Women shop almost every day.
They know they will have to have
the money or a credit card at the ready.
Why don't they?
I always have my money ready.
I have found the 11th most annoying thing.

NOW YOU SEE ME

In line at the supermarket, the lady
behind me hits me with her cart and says,
"Oh, I am so sorry. I didn't see you."
I reply, "That's because I was invisible,
but when you hit me, I became visible."

HOW TO MAKE ELDERLY PEOPLE HAPPY

You meet an elderly person or
have an elderly person in your family,
and you notice one glaring thing:
that elderly person is sad
most of the time.
Oh, that person may have some
happy moments, but they
don't last long.
What to do? What to do?
You need to get them to talk
about their life.
You will see the light appear
in their eyes
remembering many good things
they did or were a part of.
Just make sure you have the time
to listen
because this
may take a while.

CONTROLLING DREAMS

Have you ever
tried to control
your dreams?
There I was flying
all over when
this happened:
I realized I was
dreaming.
I started to fall
and woke up.
Bummer.
There must be a way
to correct this and
stay in the air.
So far I keep falling
and waking up.
Bummer!

CONVERSATION WITH AN ALIEN

Me: So you are here again.
Alien: We were always here.
Me: I have heard something like that before.
Are you us?
Alien: We used to be.
Me: And now?
Alien: You will become us, in time.
Me: One big happy family, eh?
Alien: Something like that.
Me: When will the change take place?
Alien: It started years ago.
Me: The contrails?
Alien: In part.
Me: Will we be destroyed?
Alien: No. You are us. We are you.
Me: Can this be stopped?
Alien: No. Me: What's the end game? Why all this?
Alien: We are going home. Moving back,
you might say.

LIFESAVERS

Medical people, policemen, firemen
save lives all the time.
But there is someone else
who saves a life
every day.
It's you.
You save your life every minute
of every day.
Think about that.
Be careful out there.

EMOTIONS

You want to see
honest-to-goodness
happiness or sadness?
People with real
emotions
wet or dry?
Then go sit in an airline
boarding area.
You will not
be disappointed.
When I traveled,
I saw it all.
You will too.

PONY EXPRESS CARRYSIMPLE PLAN TO GET

(Item) A to where it's going,
providing I am not in any hurry.
A needs to go to Station 5.
I am at Station 1 and
carry A to Station 2.
When I need to go to Station 3,
I will pick A at Station 2
and leave it at Station 3.
When I need to go to Station 4,
I pick A at Station 3
and take it to Station 4.
And so on. See?
I call it the Pony Express Carry.
I don't know if I am making it up
or if this plan is already in existence.
I just know I use it. Really helps
when the item is heavy and I am not
in any hurry. Or
if I am too lazy to go to the End Station,
whatever number that happens to be.

MAKING A WILL

In my later years I find
that I must make a Will.
The hardest part is deciding
Who will get all?
Should it be only one person
or several to obtain
complete ownership?
In the meantime I am making
a list of dos and don'ts
to make things easier when he/she
or they take over.
No one gave me such a list
and I muddled along
as best I could.
I did make a list of people
to go to when things need
to be repaired or built.
Is that enough?
Maybe a little muddling along will
actually help them
as it did me.

VIBRATIONS

It has been said we are all
vibrations,
but ones that talk
and move around.
Consider for a moment:
You harmonize with a song
you like,
and you become one
with the song vibration.
Aren't you one too?
You cannot move away
from this.

SINGING

I know I cannot sing.
But when I sing to my inner voice
I sound perfect.
All the right notes are hit
and the melody lives within me.
Yet to vocalize my singing . . .
well, it's a disaster.
How do the good singers
match their inner voice
to their outer one
and create a song
I will never be able to sing
out loud correctly?

FINISHED POEMS

I wrote some poems
over the years
and pored over them
correcting, adjusting
for clarification.
I would like to send them
to be published.
But then I had the thought
some needed more
correcting and adjusting
to clear up some things.
For those of us
who write poems
we know a poem
can always use some
taking out or putting in,
because we know a poem
is really never finished.
If I did send them off
and they were published and then later saw
some glaring errors, what do I do?

A FAVOR FROM GOD

I ran across an elderly gentleman
who told me a secret.
He said when he was 9-years old
he asked God to allow him
a quiet life.
I said, "Why would you ask that
when you were only 9-years old?"
He replied, "I really don't know,
It just came to me to ask."
"And was it granted?"
"Yes," was his reply.
So what has all this to do with you?
Go out and find a 9-year old who
may need a favor from God.
But the 9-year old cannot tell you
what that favor is.
It will work better that way.
Oh, that elderly gentleman also said
it will only work for 9-year olds.

ONE MORE ROUND OF POEMS

LOOKING BACK

Many say they sometimes look back
on their lives.
Some say they thought they were someone
very special and that everything would be a breeze.
Then life took over and struggles ensued
from time to time.
After a long while, "very special" lost to the pedestal
and "I'm just okay" found the platform.
However, some still believe that being just okay
is okay,
but others are always looking for the day
when they can become that very special person
in real time and not just
in their minds.
Hey, it could happen.

THE LETTER

Not sure how this happened, but
I received a letter from me.
Me?
Yes, me.
The letter asked how I was and hoped all was good with
and for me.
Well, I couldn't lie (to me) and I was going
to reply things could be better.
And I am sure that I (me) would understand.
But here's the thing: things could be a LOT better,
and I (me) could help me much better than before.
Now how can I tell me what to do?
Should I reply?

WE WERE 9

We were 9 at work.
Now we are 5.
All 9 were the team,
and all inspired each other.
Recently, we lost 4, and
the 9 are less for losing the 4,
but we don't feel the loss
because the 4 will always be with us.
That's just the way it is and
will be.
The 9 will always live on
as long as 1 is left.
And when the 1 is gone
The 9 will be together,
linked again.
That's just the way it is and
will be.
Long live the 9.

HUMAN RULES

1. Do no harm to yourself or to others.
2. Do no harm to yourself or to others.
3. Do no harm to yourself or to others.
4. Do no harm to yourself or to others.
5. Do no harm to yourself or to others.
6. Do no harm to yourself or to others.
7. Do no harm to yourself or to others.
8. Do no harm to yourself or to others.
9. Do no harm to yourself or to others.
10. Do no harm to yourself or to others.

THE PATH

We may not realize it, but
we have to wait for that special person
to cross our path.
Is it all part of some Plan in the Universe
or is it haphazard?
Love at first sight?
Yes, only if that person is on the Path.
Otherwise, forgetaboutit.
Now who or what puts that special person
on our Path?
That's the question we need an answer to.
But if we do meet and connect with that person
on our Path,
Do we still have Free Will?

GOLF

With winter almost gone and
the warmer weather slowly creeping in
to replace the cold,
I plan to play more golf this year.
I say that every year, and
this time, I really mean it.
Of course, I also say that every year.
We'll see . . .

RECURRING DREAMS

Most of us have recurring dreams.
We do not know why.
We do not know what triggers them.
In my case I have 2-dreams that occur often.
One is always the same, nothing changes.
The other is different as more scenes
are added, almost like a story with a beginning,
middle, and maybe an ending?
And it is here that I wonder what is going on.
Am I being told something?
Is there a message in this dream I must comply with?
But here's the thing:
This dream has nothing to do with any past life experience
in my conscious past.
Does my subconscious have a life of its own that
I know nothing about?

A SENIOR MOMENT

A senior moment is a moment in time
when we fall into an abyss and
have no idea that we are in it.
We just go about our business as if
nothing has happened.
Then someone tells us we had a
senior moment.
At first we think that is a good thing, and
after the laughter dies down, we see
that is not the case.
What to do? What to do?
Laugh a little with them and tell them
what they have to look forward
to in time.

WHATEVER HAPPENED TO . . .

Body by Fisher?
Where did they go?
Can't they see that the cars
of today all look alike, and
something must be done.
The Body by Fisher people
gave us beautiful, distinctive,
stylish, and classic-looking designs.
Where did they go?
The cars of today can only be
recognized by the logos and from
a distance, it's hard to tell
what is what.
Where did Body by Fisher go?
Bring them back.

ATTRACTION

Many of us are attracted to gold, silver,
diamonds, various jewels, and many more,
things too numerous to mention here.
As for me, I am seriously attracted to
shiny silver to such a point I have to catch
my breath.
Why? Why is this so?
The thought goes through my mind that I want
to be that silver and become one with it.
Was I that silver in the past
and long to go back?
Is silver the magnet that attracts me
the way others are attracted to other metals,
jewels, and so on?
Something to think about.

BRAD PITT

Who would I want to see Brad Pitt play in a movie?
The Lone Ranger, Capt. Kirk, Superman.
The Lone Ranger? Problem:
I would also want Brad to play Tonto.
The kids would cry, "Who?" Hmmm . . .
What to do? What to do?
Capt. Kirk? No, I would want Brad
to play Spock as well. Hmmm . . .
Superman?
We'd have to dye Brad's hair black.
I don't think he would mind.
I mean it's not forever.
Maybe Brad has some ideas.
Should I call him?
I still have his number
I found in one of the tabloids.
Should still be good.

HER NAME IS ABRIEL

Inspired by Abriel

She tells others to call her Abbi.
I told her to tell others to call her Abriel.
I reminded her that her parents lovingly
gave her the name Abriel,
and that is what they want to hear.
However, I said she could tell close friends
to call her Abbi, but only
close friends.
Otherwise her name is Abriel.

GROUNDHOG DAY

Every day is Groundhog Day.
It repeats every 24/7.
The sun comes up,
clouds fill the sky,
the wind makes presence known,
and night is the second half.
Wrinkles sometimes abound:
Rain, snow, fog, and hail, but
the day is still the day.
Will it always be so?

THINGS I HAVE HIDDEN

I put things away so they are not in the way
as I go about important business.
One day I needed to weigh myself
before going to my appointment
Just to see how well I did following
the steps outlined for me.
Well, I couldn't do it.
The scale was nowhere to be found.
Now it's not a small item, and
one would think I would come across it
easily enough.
Didn't happen.
Yes, there is a part of me that didn't want
to find it.
You see my subconscious protects me
from embarrassing truths.

SUPERPOWERS

I had a dream whereby a Voice
told me I was selected to receive superpowers.
I asked, "You mean like Clark Kent?"
Voice: Who?
Me: Never mind, why am I chosen?
Voice: To save the world.
Me: Why can't you do it?
Voice: We cannot. If we did the other 7-nations
would not believe us and think it was one of them
pulling a fast one. Nothing would get done.
Me: Yes, but why me?
Voice: This is where we landed.
Me: When will I get these powers?
The dream ended but not before I heard, "Soon."
I am certain that is what I heard . . .
. . . Am positive . . .
. . . Am sure . . .
. . . Pretty sure.

TIMING

I thought we were good, but
she said it wasn't working out,
the timing wasn't right
Timing?
What is that?
Oh, she meant to say "her timing."
Now where does that
leave me?
Did I just answer my own
question?

CONFESSION

Many of us go to confession
to ward off going to hell.
Back in the day, priests were known
to run someone out of the church
for eating meat on a Friday.
As for other parts, priests always
wanted to know, "How many times?"
Was there a limit?
Today, it's different,
but the memories are still there
when things were
not so relaxed.
That's why confession is still
a tentative thing.

WELL-MEANING FRIENDS

Some of us have well-meaning friends who
are the first to say: I told you so, not to buy it,
not to loan the money, and so on.
Of course, most of the time they seem to be right.
No argument here.
We did what we did because at that moment in time,
it was the right thing to do.
Do we feel bad and wished we had taken their advice?
Yes, because we know these friends were right, sort of.
And **yes again** because we did get hurt, and
our friends don't want to see that in us.
No, because at that moment in time, that was the right thing to do.
Wasn't this made clear earlier?

GOOD DRIVER

My brother Gary was a good driver.
He didn't do foolish things behind the wheel,
and he obeyed all traffic rules.
When someone was too impatient and wanted
to pass him, he let them, of course.
To no one in general, but actually to that driver,
Gary would say, "See you at the light."
And most of the time, he did.

PREMONITION

In a recent dream, I was on a bus near the driver.
We were about to round a curve to the right.
The driver was doing something else, and his hands
were nowhere near or on the wheel.
I rushed up to his right side and tried to turn
the wheel to the left to stay on the road.
I was too late, and we went over the side.
The dream ended as we were in midair.
Are we given hints or signs about our deaths
and sometimes do not know it, or if we do,
do we keep silent about it?
If I die going over a cliff, I would say
that all of us do get an idea of how we will die.
So now you have something
to think about . . . look forward to.

THE VOICE

I clearly hear a Voice telling me to "Wake Up."
I was still tired and wanted to go back for a bit.
The Voice did not sound human and not metallic,
but it was clear that it wanted me to wake up.
Did I get up?
Of course, as I was given the impression
that something bad would happen to me
if I didn't get up because it sounded threatening.
Why was I told to wake up at that time?
I kept waiting for a signal or something to explain
everything the rest of the day.
Here's the thing:
nothing happened the rest of the day.
All was quite normal.
The only thing I can guess is that whoever
I saw that day needed to see me and interact with me.
I may have been a catalyst for something unknown to me.
This is called LIFE, and no one can explain it.
What will I hear tomorrow morning?
Who or what was that Voice?

BULLETPROOF

Humans are not bulletproof, but
there comes a time,
in a young man's life,
when that special girl looks and smiles
at that young man,
who just asked her out on a date,
and she says, "yes"
that he truly feels as though he is
indeed, bulletproof.
Indeed.

HANDYMAN

Contractors would come into the yard
and see my uncle and me working on something.
They would approach me first and talk to me, as though
I was the owner
and that my uncle was my handyman.
Of course, I would correct them and send them
over to my uncle.
Later on, I would tell uncle that the contractor
thought he was my handyman.
Uncle would laugh and continue working.
In time, I am sure I will become the "handyman"
when a contractor makes contact
with a younger family member
working with me.

THE BEGINNING

There is a quest to determine
the beginning of TIME.
As some scientists believe
that will finally resolve everything
they now question.
How silly.
Don't they see the T?

NICE DREAM

Something nice happened
last night.
I had a dream about my dream girl.
I saw her better than I was able to see
her in real life.
How was that possible?
I have no clue, but there she was
as pretty and innocent as a spring day.
The dream didn't last long,
but she did look in my direction.
Does that mean she does notice me too?
Does she know that I worship her?
Probably not,
but now I have to ask:
Do I show up in her dreams?

LIFE

Life is a moment
multiplied.

A STATUE OF GILDA RADNER

A statue needs to be erected to
Gilda Radner.

She has been the most prophetic
of all comedians ever.
Her mantra was, "It's always something"
for things expected and unexpected.
And if truth be told, her mantra is now
our mantra.
Where should the statue be erected?
Simple, next to the Statue of Liberty.
Why?
To let everyone know they came here
to be free, but there will be times
when expected and unexpected things happen,
and the cry will go up:
"It's always something,"
Thank you, Gilda Radner.

A PONY

Back in the day, on the radio, the Lone Ranger
Show had a contest whereby a kid could win a pony.
All we had to do was to color Silver from a cereal box,
and send it in.
I guess the best coloring won.
I colored Silver and gave my parents my artwork
and the address where to send it.
My parents must have cringed every 24/7.
That is, if they sent it in.
I am sure they reasoned they could not
afford a pony that ate like a horse, resided in an
expensive stall, and don't forget veterinarian billings.
Meanwhile, I knew I would win and went to the local
horse stable in town to pick out the stall for my pony.
Every day thereafter, I would ask if any mail came for me.
The answer was always no.
Looking back on my quest for a pony, my parents
must not have sent in my coloring, and today, of course, I don't
blame them.
However, I did get that decoder ring.
Look at it this way: my parents smiled when they gave it to me.
It was cheaper than a pony.

BOOK TITLES
(IF EVER PUBLISHED)

Poems, Um, Thoughts Poem Format because I Don't Like Prose
Thoughts, Um, Poems
. . . Whatever
Fun Poems, All by Design Poems for Stand-Up Material
Poems from Thoughts
Thoughts into Poems
Poems, Thoughts . . . And You Thought You Didn't Like Poetry
Whatever Skid Marks
Poems by Design No Rhyme or Reason Poetry
Poems of Sorts
Poems of Sorts and by Design Anyone Can Write Poetry. See, I Did.
My Thoughts, My Poems Why Am I Doing This? What's the Point?
My Poems from My Thoughts
Whatever
I have no clue what to call it. May not be good enough to be published.
Need help. Whatever.

THE ORCHARD

The Orchard was once lush, filled with apples,
cherries, plums and pears,
with green leaves swaying and bees buzzing.
Then the bees were gone.
Where? No one knows.
Now, no fruit of any kind, the leaves still sway
in the wind, but no bees are seen or heard.
Why keep the trees?
Why not cut them down and produce
a fine lawn.
That's the plan;
To slowly bring the Orchard back to life
with dwarf fruit trees that will need great care.
Hopefully, some bees will see this and again
be seen and heard.
It will take some time.

QUANDARY

Q: Would you rather be able to go back in time or win a huge lottery?
Me: Knowing what I know now if I went back?
Q: Yes.
Me: How big a lottery?
Q: Huge, millions.
Me: The lottery.
Q: You sure?
Me: Yes.
Q: Why?
Me: To prevent the butterfly effect
in a bad way if I went back.

THINGS HAVE CHANGED

Now I carry a cell phone with me all the time.
I have caller ID at each phone in the house.
A computer controls my car.
I watch a big-screen TV.
My knees won't allow me to weed-whack.
I have doctor appointments.
I'm considering suspenders.
I started writing poems.
Golf is now something I watch on TV.
Tennis is now something I watch on TV.
Now I am Type 2.
Exercise is something others do.
I take my own trash to the landfill.
Movies are better with CGI.
My memory isn't what it used to be.
My memory isn't what it used to be.
I do movie reviews for friends.
I play lotteries every week.
But friends and family have never changed.
They are my lottery win.

2 THINGS

There are 2 things that we simply
cannot get away from.
One is fight movies as one comes along
almost every 2 minutes.
The other is learning someone visited
Heaven and came back.
By the law of averages, I predict that
most of us will also visit Heaven
and return and tell the rest of us
what awaits us there.
Until that happens, we wait
and watch the latest fight movie.

QUESTIONS

As we go along in life,
we learn that those who have passed
have the answers to most of our questions.
For some reason, we don't think of those questions
until it's too late.
To avoid all this think about your family and what
everyone did at certain times,
think hard and write down your questions
while those members are still here.
As for me, there is only one question I need
the answer to: Alas, it's now too late, but the question
to my uncle would have been:
"Where did you hide the money?"

STILL MORE POEMS

BUCKET LIST

People who say they have
a bucket list
are really telling people
what they want to do
in the future to make
their lives "complete."
How silly.
Being true to oneself
is the only list
anyone needs.

MY HOBBY

My hobby is looking for and finding
money on the ground.
My goal is to find at least
one dollar during one year.
I reason that if I can find
one dollar during the year
250 million people in the US
can do the same.
And this leads me to believe that
over the course of a year,
$250 million or more
lies on the ground throughout
the USA.
Got your attention now?

THE LOOK

You look at me
as though your eyes
are telling me
to do something.
I watch your eyes
and see a thinking process.
What are you thinking about?
·Your next meal?
·Where to go to rest?
·Some alone time?
No, I think it's about
your next meal, and
you wish I would go away
and get it ready for you.
It's always about
your next meal.
Your eyes told me
what you are thinking,
dear cat.

THE BEST THING IN THE WORLD

There I was on a hot August day
putting shingles on an already hot, burning roof.
I am sweating streams
down my face, back, and legs.
There doesn't seem to be any relief
on this very hot, humid, low-cloud day.
Taking a break can't happen for a while.
What to do? What to do?
And then it happens:
a cool breeze out of nowhere,
and it hits the spot. Wow!
I linger and strain my neck higher, hoping
to expose more area.
Where it comes from, I don't care.
But why it comes is a mystery.
I mean, this day brings a dying kind of heat.
Why indeed?
But let's face it: it is the best thing in the world.
My work picks up, and I hope
another cool breeze comes along.
And right now, I no longer care about
the why.

WHAT WE OWN

When we die
we give up all those items
we had rented: land, house,
money, stocks, etc.
We never owned them,
we just rented.
Then when we die we give
all those items to other renters.
There are only two things
we actually, positively own:
our health and our memories.

MY EPITAPH

When expected and unexpected things happen, comedienne Gilda Radner used to say, "It's always something." I agree and that led me to think about my epitaph.
Thanks to Gilda Radner, I have decided the following will be put on my tombstone:
Always something. NOW THIS.

LOTTERY DREAMS

Dreams mean nothing.
If one reads too much into dreams
one is simply dreaming wishfully.
I have dreamed I won a big lottery
3-times.
Have I won in real life?
No.

TABLOIDS

My mother used to bring
home the tabloids from
where she worked.
Years ago, on a visit,
I couldn't find the Globe,
Star, Inquirer
and asked where they were.
She said she didn't bring them
home anymore.
I said, "Well, then how are we
going to know what is really
going on in the world?"

LOTTERIES

Sure, I play the lotteries.
I don't spend the money
I used to, but as long as I
am in, I am fine.
Then this thought hit me like a ton of bricks:
suppose I only won a very small
lottery jackpot?
Sure, I would be happy
with it, but does that mean
I will never win a big jackpot?
Hmmm . . . I play to win
a very big jackpot, but it's possible
I will get only a small lottery with a small jackpot.
To counter that, I would then
only play when it's a very big jackpot.
But . . . I just can't do it.
I need to be in all draws
Because one never knows,
does one?

FINGERNAILS

Inspired by a bee sting

Yes, fingernails look nice.
Women clean, snip, shape,
and color them.
But for the man, the fingernails
only mean one thing.
They are the perfect
scratchers.

LEFT-HAND TURNS

On an errand, Uncle tells me
I passed the places we were going to.
I said, We'll get them on the way back.
Right now, they are left-hand turns, and to make
another left turn into oncoming traffic
is insane.
On the way back, we went to the places
we were going to and only made
right-hand turns.

ONIONS

On my way back from the grocery store,
I realized I forgot the onions.
In line again, the cashier says,
"See you are back."
I replied, "Yes, before there was a lady
in the produce section with very short
dress, and that threw me off my game."
The cashier says, "Life can be tough sometimes."
I agree and go home.

MY HAWAIIAN VACATION

A new car was bought and we were on our way
across the USA to Hawaii via USAF Space A.
We stopped at my aunt's house in California.
Her first words to me, "I am so glad you are here.
You can help us drive to New York." Bummer.
I helped drive my Hawaiian friend to San Francisco
to drop him and the car off. I took a bus back to my aunt's house
and spent a few days in their pool as they were
getting ready for the NY trip.
While in the pool, my aunt asked me about snakes
that may come down from the nearby hills surrounding
the pool in the backyard.
I told her the snakes are more afraid of her than she was
of them. She appeared to have bought it.
Then off we went, my aunt, her kids, and me. My uncle would
meet them in NY after his meetings.
We enjoyed a very pleasant time in the air-conditioned car,
getting off the road by 3-pm each day, staying at very good motels,
and having meals to die for. It was great.
They dropped me off at the Port Authority in New York while they
went on to Long Island and I took a bus back to Dover AFB, DE.
And that was my Hawaiian vacation. HA!

FREE WILL

Most people think we have Free Will
due to a religious leaning or belief.
I am sure there is that to contend with, but
the real reason we have Free Will
is to allow all people of the entire world to be
creative, to build things, write great literature,
invent that which needs inventing, and so on.
Without Free Will, nothing would be done.
Nothing.
Absolutely nothing and
civilization would not progress.

THE VIEW

We cut down a huge arborvitae tree
that was blocking our view of the outlying
landscape showing gentle rolling hills
and good-sized trees.
What we discovered shocked us.
We counted 9 bird nests.
And when these nests hit the ground,
they didn't break up.
They were solid structures.
We made some birds homeless.
Of course, the birds will rebuild . . . somewhere else, and
we did make them homeless for a bit,
but now we have a really nice view.

MY DOCTOR IS RETIRING

Learned that my doctor
is retiring.
Bummer. Not good.
At my last appointment,
I told him he could only retire
under 2 conditions:

·He reaches 85 yrs of age
·He outlives all of his patients

whichever comes first.
Works for me. HA!

LUGGAGE

Inspired by Mike Z

Mike told me he bought a piece of luggage.
When he opened it, he found $250
in a hidden–so to speak-compartment.
All the tags were still on the item.
Mike figures someone bought and used
the bag for a one-time thing
and returned the bag to the store
but forgot about the money.
Mike said the person thought he was
screwing the store but got screwed instead.
Mike says there is justice in the world after all.
But there is a lesson here:
When you buy luggage, check it out.
I mean, really check it out.
Ya never know . . .
However, if you are looking for a moral
to this story:
If you find any money in luggage you bought,
contact the store manager
and see how that works out for you. HA!

PENS

I watched the cashier work very hard
to clear up the current customer.
When she was done, I said, "You don't
get too much of a break between customers, do you?
You should take some time, look something in a drawer,
or make like you dropped something on the floor
and are looking for it."
She opens a drawer and I see a lot of pens.
"Wow, you sure have a lot of pens in there."
She: Yes, but not the good one.
Me: Maybe someone walked off with it.
She: That is how I lose many good pens.
Me: That is how I get many good pens.

TV SHOWS

Recently, someone asked me
why I like the TV shows I watch.
Well, I like a good story
and like the way the cast works.
If there is the possibility of a good story,
but there is a character I do not like,
then the show is history.
In movies I may also see a character
I do not like, but this is a one-time
thing and I can live with it,
but not in a regular TV series.
In many of the drama shows I watch,
I get to see and hear a lot of good comedy.
I don't watch any TV comedy shows
as they are not funny and show
more of an interest in bathroom/bedroom
humor that falls flat.
Want to see a good comedy?
Watch a good drama show and you
will see good humor within.

YOUTH MACHINE

My friend is building a Youth Machine, and
I can't wait for it to be finished.
I have seen this girl, who is the prettiest
thing I have ever seen,
and this includes many movie stars.
She outshines them all.
Why do I need the Youth Machine?
I need to go back to being 20 yrs of age,
My friend says his machine will do that for me.
I am into my early 70s,
and she is 15, 16, 17, or 18 years of age.
It's hell being in my 70s,
running around with teenager eyes.
See?
Did I mention that she is very pretty?
I need to go check to see
how he is doing.

COMBS

I used to carry a comb
in my back pocket.
It would always break.
I decided to carry 2 combs.
In case one does break,
I will have the other.
Funny thing:
now neither one breaks . . . ever.
Go figure.

POEM REVIEW

Sometimes I will re-look
at a poem I had written
and wonder why in the world
did I write it.
It isn't very good, no hook,
no humor, and no real point.
But now I have to re-look
at these comments
and are they fair?
I have discovered that I must
look somewhat deeper and
put myself into the same mood
as when I first wrote the poem.
I do hope I have an "ah-ha" moment
and finally see it.
Of course, I will ask:
why didn't I see it before?
What will others see?

NO MORE

No more words on the wind;
No more songs sung;
No more going here and there;
No more working, playing, praying;
No more explaining, claiming, saying;
No more helping, juggling, snuggling;
No more loving, savoring, cherishing;
No more looking, watching, hovering;
No more winning, losing, settling;
No more fighting, arguing, hand-shaking;
No more breathing, seething, teething;
No more eating, relieving, resting;
No more buying, selling, sighing;
No more mulling, telling, dwelling;
No more sleeping, keeping, tweaking;
No more dancing, prancing, glancing;
And no more running, walking, waiting;
No more anything.
Everything stops.
This is what Death does.

HEAVEN-LIKE

Q: Why don't you want world peace?
M: It will never happen.
Q: How so?
M: Because there will still be warring factions,
and bad things will still be done to others.
Q: Then what do you want?
M: A world where everyone is nice to each other,
has respect for each other, and
no one harms anyone.
Q: Isn't that like world peace?
M: It's more than that.
Q: How so?
M: It's Heaven-like.

YET, STILL MORE POEMS

Red Sky

The Sky was red, a kind of opaque-ish red.
Some saw a face in the red sky
others saw nothing, not even the red sky.
Then, more faces appeared and still many
saw nothing, no red sky, no faces.
Was this it? Is this the end?
Or another beginning?
Now the sky was filled with faces, heads
of important departed, some long forgotten,
some not.
This all happened in the morning
and sailors knew the meaning.
They always knew.
Some of us became sailors and still others
saw nothing.
We shouldn't be allowed to dream
such dreams, but we have no choice in this.

KIDS TODAY

As a kid, I watched all kinds of cowboy
shows in movies and on TV.
It was with these cowboys, my role models,
that I truly learned about good and bad
because in those shows,
I saw the consequences
of doing bad and of always doing good.
So I continually thank Roy, Gene, Hoppy et al.
I often wish that today's kids could learn
those lessons too.
However, friend Jeff told me that it won't happen
because today's kids do not have the attention span
needed to watch those slow moving stories.
Today's kids want everything fast and now.
Sad, isn't it?
Where will a kid today learn and see
consequences without becoming a bad one?
Huh?

THE FUTURE

I stand in the Present
and look to the Future
which is one step away.
Once I take that step
I am again in the Present
and again look to the Future,
which is always one step away.
We can never stand in the Future,
but always stand in the Present.
We can only look to the Future,
but never be in it because
it doesn't physically exist.

A BLANK PAGE

A blank page tells us everything
we ever need to know
because it is here
that everything begins.
When you look at a blank page, what do you see?
I see Everything.

THE FOREVER SMILE

She smiles at everyone, but for me
she smiles that warm joyful grin
that tells me all my burdens are gone,
no pressure and I am bullet-proof.
I have no fear of the world because
that smile tells me
love will always be with us.
I see no obstacles.
I see her smile at me and
I am warm throughout.
We will be very happy:
the three of us: she, me
and that smile I like to call
The Forever Smile.

CHURCH CHANGES

First was the Mass in English -no problem.
Next: the priest faced the parishioners -no problem.
Then: the railing was removed – no problem.
They let us take Communion in the hand – no problem.
They said women didn't have to cover their heads – no problem.
Then: laymen handed out Communion -no problem.
Then: They wanted us to say Holy Spirit and not Holy Ghost -no problem
Then: Collection baskets no longer had that long pole attached – no problem
Then: 2-collection baskets came around – 2nd for special needs -no problem
Then: Laymen gave the church news from the pulpit – no problem
Then: laymen did all the readings except the Gospel – no problem.
Then: they wanted us to drink wine – no problem.
Then: they took the wine away – no problem.
Then: they made us shake hands – uncomfortable -but not a problem.
Then someone brought in a guitar for a Guitar Mass – problem but that didn't last long and now not a problem.

Later Deacons abounded – not necessary -but no problem.

Now Confessions and The Rosary are emphasized – no problem.

Also: pledges for money became frequent – some see that as a problem.

There were no changes to the story of 2000 years ago – no problem.

No change in the 2000+ year-old story is a good thing.

ALZHEIMER'S TEST

I am told that a simple test for Alzheimer's
is to recite the months of the year
in reverse order.
I can do that……………
now.

THE LOOP

I went to bed too early
woke up, couldn't sleep.
went to the computer,
began to get sleepy,
went back to the bed,
now wide awake again,
so back to the computer,
and then back to the bed,
and now wide awake.
Tried the tv, and got sleepy
so back to the bed,
and again wide awake,
and back to the computer,
and it again didn't work,
till sleepy.
After all this, one would think
I would go to the bed and pass out
from sheer exhaustion.
Didn't happen.
Am still in the Loop.

STARS

Looking at the stars is
quite an experience.
So many, so far away.
Some say we only see
the light of the stars as
the light comes to earth
and that the stars are
no longer there.
That can't be.
We need the stars
for our dreams.
I say the stars
are still there.
Let's dream…………

COFFEE

One of the best things about mornings
is a great cup of coffee to start the day.
There was a time I didn't know
which brand/blend to use.
Expresso and Latte are not considered.
Looking for a regular Joe.
There are many brands
that tout multi flavor blends.
There are: original roast, dark roast,
vanilla, French vanilla, peppermint, caramel,
banana, pumpkin, cinnamon, mocha
hazelnut, bourbon, chicory,
raspberry (ugh!), and there are numerous
breakfast and house brands/blends
and so many more.
Too many choices and I have tested some
and decided on this: the one with
the best taste to the very last drop.
Works for me.

STORIES

How many times have you heard,
"it's only a story." or "it's only a movie,"
and you go about your business
without second thoughts?
Yet, it's not just another story.
These stories have happened in real life
to real people young and old.
Keep in mind there is nothing new under the sun.
Think about that and have those
"second thoughts" mean something.
The stories we see have actually happened
at one time and this bears repeating.
So don't dismiss those stories,
and have some compassion.
for those people we will never know.
Okay, there are 2-things that ARE new under the sun:
CGI and Star Trek type stories.

GOING TO THE DENTIST

We all need to see the dentist regularly.
I have to go soon. I will, I will.
Today's dentistry is a wonder to behold:
better Novacane, ultra hi-speed drills,
and better Dentistry techniques
There is no excuse not to go.
I have to go soon. I will, I will.
It's not like before when the Novacane didn't
work the way it should have,
and the not-so-fast drills lumbered on forever and hurt like
the dickens. I can almost feel it now even after all these years.
I am reminded of my first Dentist.
He would always say, "just a little bit more"
"almost finished" "almost done"
And he would say these things over and over for about 20-minutes
And I believed him each time. Silly me.
I have to go soon. I will, I will.
There is nothing to be afraid of.
It'll be over in no time. Things are better now.
I have to go soon. I will, I will.

THINGS THAT NEED DOING

I got too much to do.
Where to start, where to start?
Do this first or that?
Can that wait?
Does this have to be done right now?
What about this? What about that?
Need to slow down and figure out this and that.
Need a system.
Now, what system? Oh, not another thing
added to this and that.
There must be an easier way.
Got it. Will do just one thing and figure
the rest out later.
Now, what should I do first?
This or that?
Here we go………………..

A SUNDAY OF YESTERYEAR

When I was a kid, a Sunday was like living
in a Ghost Town. Nothing moved, all was quiet,
stores were closed, very few cars on the road,
no one walking around anywhere.
But it was good time to visit my grandfather
who liked a glass of beer in his living room before
he went to the local Beer Garden to see his friends,
and play some shuffle-board.
He asked me if I wanted some beer and I said yes.
He told me to get it from the cellar, and I did.
We sat there sipping beer and he asked how I was
doing in school, things like that. I miss those talks.
There was nothing like them.
When I left, I asked him, "Pop, do you think
you could put some beer in the refrigerator for
next time I come over?" And he said he would. And he always did.
Now a Sunday is chaotic like any other day in the week,
always noisy, all stores are open,
the roads are jammed with cars and people are moving everywhere.
A Sunday is no longer a Ghost Town, but I remember when it was
and sipping cold beer with Pop.
I miss that Ghost Town.

BREAKING NEWS

It's 8-pm and the TV news station says:
a new medical breakthrough that can save
your life.
Details at 11.
Wait, wait, tell me now
I go to bed at 10-pm

WHO AM I?

We sometimes ask ourselves
Who AM I?
I mean really who am I?
As for me:
of course, I am part of my mother and father,
as you are also a part of your parents.
but we are also a part of everyone else -good or bad –
we had come in contact with since birth up to now.
And those we had not come in direct contact with:
movie stars, athletes and everyone else we may
have seen in pictures, newspapers, or TV/movies:
well, they have also contaminated us, hopefully,
in a good way.
But no matter, they became a part us,
and this is what made us up to this moment.
So now, I know who I am and you know who you are.
And it is true, we are all connected.
We really are.

SIGNS

Everyone of us looks for a sign
to help us make a good decision
regarding almost everything.
We look into the clouds, nature,
religion, animals and so on.
There is no place
we don't look.
We seem to need that crutch.
I think I found my sign.
It said:
Keep off the Grass.

GROUND HOG DAY?

You won't believe this.
I can hardly do so, too, but
I ran into someone who says
he has figured it all out.
He says think of the movie Ground Hog Day
and life as we know it as one big Ground Hog Day,
every day as it repeats over and over and over.
He says, think of all the peoples of the world as one person
like you saw in that movie.
I told him I think I get that, but there must be something done
to "that person" that will stop the days repeating.
He says he is still working on that.
Stay tuned.

PRAYER

I see fans watch the contest
with the game on the line.
I see them make the sign of the cross,
look to Heaven, eyes closed tightly
as if in prayer asking for divine intervention
to help their team win.
They want that field goal, the home run
that hit, that Ace and so on……………..
Wouldn't it be nice to have all these "fans"
do all those "prayers" to ask for World Peace?
And, they don't always have to be watching
a game to do it.

WEALTH

Q: Does it bother you that you
are not rich?
Me: No.
Q: The rich have so much and can do
many more things with their money.
Me: I know, it still doesn't bother me.
Q: Very curious.
Me: I am quite content with what I have,
and I have something they also have,
and I can wait for the fruits so to speak.
Q: What is that?
Me: Hope.
Q: Hope? How is that?
Me: They hope they don't lose their wealth.
I hope I will get wealth.
Q: So you and the rich have something in common?
Me: Yes, sort of.

THE PONYTAIL

She is a ponytail girl,
pretty, always smiling,
happy, friendly,
eyes twinkling with
a nice bounce in her steps.
She is a delight to all,
but when she is down,
she has a fear that she is not so pretty.
Then she remembers to arrange
her hair into a ponytail because
she believes that makes her pretty again.
It doesn't, as she is always pretty.
We all have that one thing
that helps make us more suitable to the world,
or so we believe.

MOTIONS

Let's face it, when we were young we went thru motions,
and not really understanding them, but we did them anyway.
Sometimes we would say, "I love you."
and really not sure if we meant it.
It was just a means to an end.
Looking back now on all those times we ask ourselves:
What was I thinking?'
The problem was always that we didn't think at all.
Was there any one time that we said to ourselves: this is it,
she is the one, I don't care about anything else but being with her?
Probably not, and looking back again there might have been one that
we would have thought that way about.
Not then, but what about now?
Ooops, too late

BELIEF

When I was a boy I believed in Santa Claus.
I would watch the night-sky in my room for a long time.
Once when I woke up on Christmas Eve and had to use the bathroom
near the stairway, I heard muffled voices downstairs and the
rustling of paper from the living room.
I knew what they were doing.
I went back to my room and looked out at the sky again.
I did this for a long, long time.
I still wanted to believe.

THOSE WHO HELP

I know and believe those dearly departed up above
who are allowed to look down
have a hand in helping me or at other times
letting me know I did something wrong or
about to or even think something I shouldn't.
How do I know and believe this?
They allow me to jam a finger,
stub a toe, open a door on my face,
bruise an elbow or, mis-step and fall
to name just a few.
Yes, they do help a lot and I am
grateful, but they don't let me get cocky or smug.
When I forget they are there to help
they have their ways of reminding me that
a jammed finger or a bruised knee is not pleasant.
Now, you may say I just have to be more
careful and watch what I do.
I try my best, but they win
every time.

LOOKING AT ME

I looked at my face in the mirror.
Looked hard, really hard…… all over.
What did I see?
    -a younger me in there?
    -an older me in there?
Or did I see neither young nor old?
What do others see?
Surely, not a younger me, but maybe the other?
That's sad. Really sad.
What can I do to change that?
Exercise, change diet?
Well, it's worth a shot……………..
Seriously, it's worth a shot.
Seriously…………………..

LOOKING

I look at you and
see me.
You look at me and
you say you see me,
That's not possible.
Look harder

A VERY HAPPY MOMENT

We all have happy moments,
and some we remember fondly.
But what if you got a happy moment
you never thought you would have?
Here's the thing:
My cowboy heroes were (still are)
Roy Rogers and Gene Autry.
In those days when they were popular
you never saw them together.
You weren't sure they liked each other.
In Biloxi, MS, one late night I turned on the TV.
And what I saw brought tears to my eyes.
Roy and Gene sitting in comfortable chairs
hosting a Tex Ritter movie.
and their banter was pure gold.
I sat mesmerized totally surprised and
privileged to see my heroes,
who apparently did like each other.
How good is that?

THE ANSWERS

They were in front of us all the time.
Most of us didn't know where to look,
until now.
It was just Nature's way of hiding
everything in plain sight.
What? You still don't know?
You are not listening.]

IMPORTANT WORDS

The two most important words
in life are:
Hope and Trust.
We all hope things will turn out right.
and we need to trust each other so
hope has a chance.

THE 4-CYL ENGINE

A 4-cyl engine strains at 65 and over.
It's okay for a 6 or an 8, but not for a 4.
The 4 is too small and it gives good
performance until it is asked to go over 65.
At 65, it will hum for a while and be okay, but
feels better when it's below 65.
At 65, the 4-cyl knows it will be stretched
in just a small matter of time,
and it hopes the water and oil levels are correct
as the only defense it has are the temp/oil gauges;
and the hope is that they are looked at often.
Who is this driver who seems to know better
than the 4-cyl?
When will he ever learn?

TYING SHOES

As a kid the hardest thing to learn
was tying our shoes.
Very confusing and we knew
it simply couldn't be done.
We would try, try and try with tears
streaming down
as it didn't matter if we could not see
our progress.
It just couldn't be done.
Then after years of trying
it happened
The shoes were tied.
How did that happen?
Now the question:
can we do it again?

About the Author

Bob is a transplanted New Yorker who now lives in Virginia. He has a BS in business management from Concord College, Athens, West Virginia. He served four years in the USAF, worked overseas in Saudi Arabia for 9.5 years, and later recruited for overseas military contracts. He still writes poems that rhyme or not but also does movie reviews—but not horror movies—for friends who need to know what their kids can watch, and he also puts the reviews on IMDb.com

www.ingramcontent.com/pod-product-compliance
Ingram Content Group UK Ltd.
Pitfield, Milton Keynes, MK11 3LW, UK
UKHW022227230426
12048UKWH00016BA/1111